Finding Strength In God's Word

A 30 Day Devotional

Maddie T. Kabba

D & G Publishing LLC

TABLE OF CONTENTS

INTRODUCTION

Welcome to *"Finding Strength in God's Word,"* a 30-day journey designed to help you explore the concept of strength from a biblical perspective. Whether you are feeling physically, emotionally, or spiritually weak, we believe this devotional will offer you encouragement and hope as you seek to grow in your faith and reliance on God.

Throughout these 30 days, we will examine various aspects of strength and how they relate to our walk with God. We will explore topics such as seeking direction for strength, the role of fellowship in finding strength, the power of joy and renewal in strengthening us, and the importance of trusting in God's strength. We will also delve into the challenges of finding strength in times of trial, the idea that God's strength is made perfect in weakness, and how God's hand of strength can support and sustain us.

In addition to reflecting on these themes through prayer and reading God's Word, we encourage you to seek fellowship with others as you journey through this devotional. Whether through a small group, a mentor or accountability partner, or simply a trusted friend, having supportive relationships can make a big difference in our ability to find strength and courage in times of challenge.

We pray that this devotional will be a source of encouragement and strength for you as you seek to grow in your faith and reliance on God. May you experience the fullness of his love, grace, and power as you trust in him for strength and guidance.

DAY 1: STRENGTH BY FOLLOWING HIS COMMANDS

"Therefore shall ye keep all the commandments which I command you this day, that ye may be strong, and go in and possess the land, whither ye go to possess it" - Deuteronomy 11:8

This passage speaks to the experience of the children of Israel, who, when they followed God's commands, could conquer even the strongest nations and pass through the Red Sea. However, as time passed and they strayed from God's commandments, they began to suffer defeats from even the smallest nations.

This passage suggests that our strength comes from obedience to God's word. When we follow His direction, we are refreshed and able to accomplish the tasks He has set before us. On the other hand, when we go against His direction, we are left exhausted and weak, as we are left to fend for ourselves.

The Kingdom of God is not a democracy; it is a monarchy with a King. His word is final. As believers, we must understand that our strength comes from following God's commands and living according to His will. When we seek to do this, we can trust in His strength to lead and guide us on the path He has set before us.

But why is obedience to God's commands so important? It is clear that obedience brings blessings, and disobedience brings curses. When we follow His commands, we align ourselves with His purpose and plan for our lives. By doing so, we position ourselves to receive the blessings He has promised to those who follow Him. In Deuteronomy 28, God spells out the blessings that will come to those who obey His commands and the curses that will come to those who do not.

In addition to the blessings that come with obedience is our relationship with God. When we obey God's commands, we show Him that we love Him and are willing to follow Him. This strengthens our connection with Him. On the other hand, disobedience hurts our relationship with Him.

In summary, the importance of obedience to God's commands cannot be overstated. Our strength comes from following His direction and living according to His will. When we seek to do this, we can trust in His strength to lead and guide us and expect to receive the blessings He has promised to those who follow Him. May we strive to obey God's commands, putting Him first in our lives and seeking to honor and glorify Him in all we do.

Prayer:
Dear Lord,
Please order my steps and guide me on the path you have for me. Please help me be obedient to your commands, as I know my strength comes from following your direction. Empower me to live a life that is pleasing to you and brings honor and glory to your name. I understand that obedience is not just about following rules but about seeking to live a life surrendered to your will. Please help me to put you first in my life and to seek your will above all else. Please bless me with the strength and guidance I need to follow your commands and live a life that is pleasing to you. Thank you for your faithfulness and your goodness.
In Jesus' name, I pray,
Amen.

READING: Deuteronomy 11:1-32.

Reflection: How has disobedience to God's commands affected you in the past?

What specific blessings have you received due to your obedience to God's commands?

In what areas of your life do you struggle with obedience to God's will?

How can you prioritize obedience to God in your daily life?

How can you strengthen your relationship with God through obedience to His commands?

DAY 2: DIRECTION FOR STRENGTH - PART 1

"And David enquired at the LORD, saying, Shall I pursue after this troop? Shall I overtake them? And he answered him, Pursue: for thou shalt surely overtake them, and without fail recover all." - *1 Samuel 30:8.*

David and his army were returning from war to find that the Amalekites had raided their cities and taken their families, possessions, and children. The people were devastated and even considered stoning David. Amid this crisis, David sought guidance from the Lord, asking if he should pursue the Amalekites and if he could overtake them. The Lord answered, promising David would overtake Amalekites and recover all they had looted.

This assurance from God gave David strength. He pursued the Amalekites with only four hundred soldiers and defeated them.

This passage illustrates the power of seeking guidance from the Lord and following His direction. When we ask the Lord what to do and which way to go, He will give us the strength and ability to accomplish the tasks He has set before us. Even in times of disappointment and hardship, we can find strength by turning to the Lord and following His leadership.

This passage also emphasizes the importance of seeking guidance from the Lord in our decision-making. Rather than relying on our understanding, we can turn to the Lord for direction and trust in His guidance. When we follow His lead, we can be assured that He will enable us to overcome any challenges that may come our way. Let us seek the Lord's direction in all things and trust His strength to guide and empower us on the path He has set before us.

Prayer:
Dear Lord, I come to you today seeking strength and
direction for my life. I know that Your Word is a source of
strength and guidance for me, and I ask that you reveal a
specific Word that will provide me with the strength and
direction I need today. By Your Holy Spirit, I ask that you
speak to my heart and give me a Word that will encourage
and strengthen me in my walk with you. Help me
understand the meaning of this Word and apply it to my
life in a way that brings honor and glory to your name.
I trust in your goodness and faithfulness to guide and direct
my steps. I pray that you will use this Word to bring clarity
and purpose to my life and help me live in a way that is
pleasing to you.
In Jesus' name, I pray,
Amen.

READING: 1 Samuel 30:1-8

Reflection:

How have you experienced the power of seeking guidance from the Lord in your own life?

In what situations do you struggle to turn to the Lord for guidance and direction?

How has the Lord given you strength and ability to accomplish tasks He has set before you?

How has seeking guidance from the Lord helped you to overcome challenges and disappointments?

In what areas of your life can you prioritize seeking the Lord's direction and trusting in His guidance?

DAY 3: DIRECTION FOR STRENGTH - PART 2.

"The LORD is my shepherd; I shall not want. He restoreth my soul: he leadeth me in the paths of righteousness for his name's sake" - Psalms 23:1 - 3.

This passage speaks to the importance of God as our guide and shepherd. When we follow His direction, we can trust in His power and provision to see us through any challenges that may come our way.

One of the critical causes of emotional and physical exhaustion is misdirection in life. When we try to have our way, we often struggle to make progress, which can be very tiring. On the other hand, when we follow God's plan and allow Him to lead us, we can trust in His strength and guidance to see us through.

In life's journey, it is essential to recognize that God's plan is always better than our own. When we seek His direction and follow His ways, we can enjoy the benefits of His power and provision. Let us turn to the Lord as our shepherd and trust His guidance to lead us in righteousness.

Prayer:
Dear Heavenly Father,
I come to you today recognizing that Your ways are higher than mine. I confess that I have often tried to have my way but have ended up feeling exhausted and drained.

I ask that You order my steps and guide me in the path that You have for me. Help me to trust in Your lead and follow Your direction. I pray that You will give me the strength and energy I need to fulfill the tasks that You have set before me.

When I follow Your ways, I can trust in Your power and provision to see me through any challenge that may come my way. I pray that You would use Your Word and Your Holy Spirit to guide me and give me the strength I need to live a life that is pleasing to You.
In Jesus' name, I pray,
Amen.

READING: Psalms 23:1-6.

Reflection:

How has following God's direction brought you strength and provision in the past?

In what ways have you experienced the negative consequences of misdirection in your own life?

How can you prioritize seeking God's plan and allowing Him to lead you daily?

How can trust in God's guidance bring peace and rest to your life?

How can you recognize and follow God's plan for your life?

DAY 4: SEEK HIM, AND HE WILL STRENGTHEN YOU.

"Yet man is born unto trouble, as the sparks fly upward. I would seek unto God, and unto God would I commit my cause: Who giveth rain upon the earth, and sendeth waters upon the fields: To set up on high those that be low; that those which mourn may be exalted to safety" - Job 5:7-11

We face challenges and struggles from the moment we are born, as evident by the fact that our hospitals are filled with innocent babies experiencing difficult medical conditions. Being born again, righteous, and holy does not guarantee that Satan will not afflict us.

Satan's goal is to wear us down and drain our strength so that we have no desire to live and fulfill God's purpose. He wants to discourage us and prevent us from living meaningful and purposeful lives. The story of Job in the Bible is a testament to this, as Job was described as a "perfect and upright man, one that feared God and hated evil," yet he still suffered greatly.

In facing these challenges, we must seek God and commit our entire lives to Him. When we do this, we can trust in His power to fight for us and to bring us to a place of peace. Nothing we give to God can die, and He will use our struggles and challenges to bring about His good purposes. By seeking God and committing to Him, we can find the strength and encouragement we need to overcome any obstacles that may come our way.

Prayer:
Dear Lord Jesus,
I come to you today admitting that I have been trying to do
things on my own, which is why I am feeling weary. I have
relied on my strength and abilities rather than seeking
Your guidance and direction.

I recognize that I need You to take the wheel of my life
and guide me in the path that You have for me. I surrender
my plans and my will to You and ask that You lead me and
give me the strength and guidance I need to live a life that
is pleasing to You.

Help me trust in Your goodness and faithfulness, and rely
on Your strength and power to see me through any
challenges that may come my way. I pray that You would
use my struggles and difficulties to bring about Your good
purposes in my life.
In Your holy name, I pray,
Amen.

READING: Job 5:1-27

Reflection:

How has seeking God and committing your cause to Him brought you strength and encouragement in the past?

In what ways do you struggle with feelings of discouragement and weariness?

How can you prioritize seeking God and committing to Him in facing challenges and struggles?

How can you trust God's power to fight for you and bring peace in difficult times?

How can you find purpose and meaning in your challenges and struggles by seeking and committing to God?

DAY 5: STRENGTH BY FELLOWSHIP - PART 1.

"They go from strength to strength; every one of them in Zion appeareth before God." - Psalms 84:7.

Psalms 84:7 tells us that those who worship in Zion, or the City of David, go from strength to strength. In the New Testament, the place of worship is the Church, which is not a physical building but a gathering of believers. When we come together as believers in fellowship, we find strength and encouragement from one another.

One of the benefits of fellowship with other believers is that it helps us increase our physical, emotional, and spiritual strength. When we join hearts with other believers, we can bear our burdens more easily because we have a community of people to support us in prayer and encouragement. The Bible tells us that one person can chase a thousand enemies, and two can put ten thousand to flight. This illustrates the power of unity and strength we can find in fellowship with others.

It is vital to prioritize fellowship with other believers to grow in strength and find support and encouragement in our faith journey. When we come together in fellowship, we can build each other up and draw strength from one another. Let us prioritize seeking out fellowship with other believers and supporting and encouraging one another in our walk with the Lord.

Prayer:
Dear Lord,
I come to you today asking for Your grace to constantly be in fellowship with Your people. I recognize the importance of coming together with other believers, and I desire to be a part of a community of believers who support and encourage one another in our faith journey.

Help me prioritize fellowship with Your people and seek opportunities to come together in worship and service. I pray that You will use these gatherings to strengthen and encourage me and help me grow in my faith.

I also pray for the unity and harmony of Your Church, that we may be one body working together to glorify Your name. I pray that You would use our gatherings to bring about Your good purposes and bring others into a relationship with You.
In Your holy name, I pray,
Amen.

READING: Psalms 84:1-12

Reflection:
How has fellowship with other believers strengthened and encouraged your faith journey?

In what ways do you struggle to prioritize fellowship with other believers?

How can you seek fellowship with other believers and build each other up in your faith?

How can you draw strength and support from your community of believers in times of challenge or hardship?

How can you actively encourage and support other believers in their faith journey?

DAY 6: STRENGTH BY FELLOWSHIP - PART 02.

"O God, thou art my God; early will I seek thee: my soul thirsteth for thee, my flesh longeth for thee in a dry and thirsty land, where no water is" - Psalms 63:1

It is important to engage in communal fellowship with other believers and to prioritize personal fellowship with God equally. This personal relationship with God gives meaning and depth to our fellowship with the Church.

David, a man after God's heart, understood the importance of personal fellowship with God. He praised and worshipped God seven times a day and prayed three times a day. This constant fellowship with God was evident in David's life. He was a strong, mighty, and courageous man who won all the battles he fought. Even when his son attempted to take the throne, David regained it because of his constant fellowship with the all-knowing and all-powerful God.

Suppose you are experiencing a time of emotional or spiritual weakness. In that case, one of the most powerful ways to find strength is to maintain constant one-on-one fellowship with God through worship, praise, thanksgiving, prayer, and studying His Word. This personal fellowship with God never fails to bring renewal and strength.

Prayer:
Dear Lord,
I come to you today asking for Your grace to maintain a deep communication line with You. I recognize the importance of personal fellowship with You and desire a close and intimate relationship with You. Help me to prioritize time with You in worship, praise, thanksgiving, prayer, and studying Your Word. I pray that You will use this time to strengthen and renew me and to help me grow closer to You. I pray that You would give me the discipline to maintain this constant communication with You and use it to bring about Your good purposes in my life. In Your holy name, I pray,
Amen.

READING: Psalms 63:1-11.

Reflection:

How has personal fellowship with God brought renewal and strength to your life?

How do you prioritize personal fellowship with God in your daily life?

How does maintaining a consistent personal relationship with God enhance your fellowship with the Church and other believers?

How can you draw on the examples of people like David to inspire and guide your fellowship with God?

How can you cultivate personal fellowship with God through worship, praise, thanksgiving, prayer, and studying His Word?

DAY 7: STRENGTH IN JOY - PART 1.

"Then he said unto them, Go your way, eat the fat, and drink the sweet, and send portions unto them for whom nothing is prepared: for this day is holy unto our Lord: neither be ye sorry; for the joy of the LORD is your strength." - Nehemiah 8:10.

Nehemiah was just a cupbearer, pouring the King's wine. But when he hears about the destruction of the wall of Jerusalem, he is deeply saddened and determined to rebuild it. The King sends him to Jerusalem to lead the rebuilding, but things do not go as planned. Nehemiah and his team face opposition from the enemies of Israel, including Sanballat and Tobiah, who try to discourage them and emotionally abuse them.

Given the circumstances, it would have been understandable if Nehemiah had given up on the rebuilding project. But he found a source of strength to carry on: the joy of the Lord.

Joy is a powerful force that can help us overcome any disappointment or obstacle. It comes from acknowledging that our Father is seated upon the throne and that He cares intimately for us.

There will always be people like Sanballat and Tobiah who try to wear us down and emotionally torment us. But the joy of the Lord is the antidote that renews our strength and enables us to keep going. Let us hold onto the joy of the Lord and let it be our source of strength in the midst of any challenges we face.

Prayer:
Dear Lord,
I come to you today asking for Your help to always focus
on You rather than on the problems I face. When I fix my
eyes on You, I can find strength and hope in any situation.
By Your Holy Spirit, help me focus on You and let the joy
of Your presence be my source of strength. Help me
remember that You are seated upon the throne and care
intimately for me. I pray that You give me the grace to
trust in Your goodness and sovereignty, even when things
do not go as planned. Help me to keep my eyes fixed on
You and to let Your joy be my strength.
In Your holy name, I pray,
Amen.

READING: Nehemiah 8:1-18 (KJV).

Reflection:

How has the joy of the Lord brought you strength in difficult circumstances?

How do you struggle to maintain joy in the face of opposition or disappointment?

How can you cultivate and prioritize joy in your daily life, despite challenges or difficulties?

How does recognizing that God is seated on the throne and cares for us bring joy and strength?

How can you draw on the example of Nehemiah to find strength in joy in your own life?

DAY 8: STRENGTH IN JOY - PART 2.

"For the kingdom of God is not meat and drink; but righteousness, and peace, and joy in the Holy Ghost." - Romans 14:17.

The Kingdom of God is primarily spiritual rather than physical. In the verse above, the word "meat" refers to food. While food and drink are important for providing physical strength to the mortal body, they do not have the power to give us emotional strength or spiritual empowerment.

It is not uncommon to find physically strong people depressed or oppressed by demons. Depression and oppression cannot be overcome by physical strength alone. What we need is the joy of the Holy Spirit, which imparts strength to our souls and helps us endure life's challenges. If you are going through difficult times and feeling depressed, consider praying to the Holy Spirit and asking for the joy of the Lord. This joy will provide you with the strength you need to keep going and overcome any obstacle that comes your way.

Prayer:
Dear Lord,
I come to you today asking for Your baptism of the Holy
Spirit. I know that the Holy Spirit imparts joy to our souls
and gives us the strength to endure life's challenges. Lord, I
confess that I have struggled to find joy and strength in my
efforts. I realize that my strength is insufficient and that I
need Your supernatural power. So today, Lord, I ask Your
Holy Spirit to come and baptize me. Fill me with Your joy
and strength, and help me experience the fullness of Your
presence in my life. I pray that You would use Your Holy
Spirit to nourish me spiritually and to help me overcome
any obstacle that comes my way.
In Your holy name, I pray,
Amen.

READING: Romans 14:1-23.

Reflection:
How can you invite the Holy Spirit to bring joy and strength into your life?

How can you use the joy of the Holy Spirit to overcome feelings of depression or oppression?

How can you share the joy of the Holy Spirit with others who may be struggling to find strength in difficult times?

How can you draw on the power of the Holy Spirit to find joy and strength in your own life?

How does recognizing that the Kingdom of God is primarily spiritual rather than physical help you to find strength in joy?

DAY 9: RENEWAL OF STRENGTH - PART 1.

"Even the youths shall faint and be weary, and the young men shall utterly fall: But they that wait upon the LORD shall renew their strength; they shall mount up with wings as eagles; they shall run, and not be weary, and they shall walk, and not faint." - Isaiah 40:30-31.

As human beings, we are made up of three parts: The Spirit, the soul, and the body. While our bodies are the least significant part of our existence, they are still important because they house our spirits and souls. We interact with the physical world through our bodies and perform various undertakings.

God's Spirit does not commune with our flesh; it communes with our spirits. God is all-powerful, and His strength is greater than anything we can gain from food or drink. When God strengthens us in our spirits, it has a positive effect on our bodies as well.

The prophet Isaiah tells us that those who wait on the Lord and seek Him in fellowship and service will renew their strength. This includes prayer, fasting, studying the Word of God, and evangelism. We can experience physical revitalization and spiritual and emotional strength when we engage in these things daily.

So if you are feeling weak or exhausted, consider seeking the Lord in prayer and through other means of fellowship and service. As you wait on Him and seek Him, you will find that He renews your strength and gives you the energy you need to persevere in your daily tasks.

Prayer:
Heavenly Father,
I come to you today with a weary heart and need strength.
I know my efforts are insufficient to sustain me, and I turn
to you as my source of strength and renewal. Lord, grant
me the zeal and determination to constantly seek and wait
on you for the renewal of my strength. Please help me find
my strength in you alone, not in my own abilities or the
things of this world. Please fill me with your Holy Spirit
and empower me to serve you with energy and passion.
Please help me to rise with wings like an eagle and to run
and not be weary, even in the face of difficult challenges.

I trust you to renew my strength and give me the energy
and vitality I need to live for you and fulfill your purposes
for my life.
In Jesus' name, I pray,
Amen.

READING: Isaiah 40:1-31.

Reflection:
How has seeking the Lord through fellowship and service brought renewal and strength to your life?

In what ways do you struggle to prioritize seeking the Lord and engaging in fellowship and service?

How can you use practices like prayer, fasting, studying the Word of God, and evangelism to seek and wait on the Lord for renewal and strength?

How does strengthening your spirit through seeking the Lord impact your physical, emotional, and spiritual well-being?
 In what specific ways can you prioritize seeking the Lord and engaging in fellowship and service daily?

Day 10: Renewal of Strength - Part 2.

"That he would grant you, according to the riches of his glory, to be strengthened with might by his Spirit in the inner man;" - Ephesians 3:16.

Maintaining spiritual strength is crucial for living a healthy and fulfilling life. Unfortunately, many people who seem physically robust and healthy often suffer premature death, which spiritual triggers can cause. These triggers can manifest in physical ailments and can be challenging to overcome without addressing the underlying spiritual issues.

The Word of God, who is spirit, can nourish and strengthen us on a spiritual level. It is vital to rely on the power of God's Word and the Holy Spirit to combat spiritual attacks and maintain inner strength. Similarly, praying in the Holy Spirit can also build inner strength and provide a defense against the forces of darkness.

To maintain spiritual strength, it is crucial to constantly seek the Holy Spirit and rely on His power to fortify us against spiritual attacks. By doing so, we can live a healthy and fulfilling life, free from the burden of spiritual weakness.

Prayer:
Heavenly Father,
We come before you today seeking a fresh infilling of your
Holy Spirit. We know that without your strength and
power, we cannot accomplish your will and fulfill our
purpose on earth. We ask that you renew our spirits and
allow us to go beyond our physical limitations, relying on
your strength and guidance in all things.

Lord, we confess that we have often tried to do things in
our strength and have become weary and discouraged. But
we know that you have promised to give us rest and renew
our strength as we wait on you. Help us draw near you in
constant fellowship and seek your face in prayer and your
Word.

We pray that your joy will fill our hearts and bring peace
to our souls, even amid difficulties and challenges. We
trust in your goodness and your plan for our lives. We ask
for your wisdom and direction in all things.
We give you all the praise and honor, Lord, and thank you
for your loving kindness and grace towards us.
Amen.

READING: Ephesians 3:1-21.

Reflection:
How has relying on the power of God's Word and the Holy Spirit brought renewal and strength to your life?

In what ways do you struggle to prioritize seeking the Holy Spirit and relying on His power in your daily life?

How can you use practices like praying in the Holy Spirit and studying the Word of God to build inner strength and defend against spiritual attacks?
How does maintaining spiritual strength impact your physical, emotional, and spiritual well-being?

In what specific ways can you prioritize seeking the Holy Spirit and relying on His power in your daily life?

DAY 11: STRENGTH FOR SERVANTS - PART 01.

"But thou, Israel, art my servant, Jacob whom I have chosen, the seed of Abraham, my friend. Fear thou not; for I am with thee: be not dismayed; for I am thy God: I will strengthen thee; yea, I will help thee; yea, I will uphold thee with the right hand of my righteousness." - Is 41:8,10

Service to God is not just about attending church or participating in religious activities. It is about actively working to further God's kingdom and bring about His will on earth, including spreading the message of salvation to others and praying for revival in the world.

God values and rewards those who actively serve Him. When we commit ourselves to His work, He equips and strengthens us to carry out His plans. This strength is not just physical but also emotional and spiritual. It is a strength that allows us to persevere through challenges and difficulties and continue to serve Him with joy and dedication.

If you want to experience this strength and endurance, consider how you can actively serve God and His kingdom. Enlist as a servant of His plan and purpose, and watch as He strengthens and empowers you to carry out His will.

Prayer:
Lord,
I want to be an active servant in Your kingdom, working towards the salvation of souls and participating in Your revival agenda. Please equip me with the strength and resources I need to fulfill this calling. Help me to understand and follow Your plan and purpose for my life. May my service bring honor and glory to Your name. Amen.

READING: Isaiah 41:1-29.

Reflection:
Reflect on your own experiences of serving God and how He has strengthened you in the process. Write down any insights or takeaways from these experiences.

Consider how you can actively serve God in your daily life. This could be through sharing the Gospel with others, praying for revival, or volunteering at your church or community. Make a plan to implement this and ask God to give you the strength and resources to carry it out.

Spend some time in prayer, asking God to show you His plan and purpose for your life and to give you the strength and endurance you need to fulfill it.

Consider finding a small group or accountability partner to support and encourage you in your journey of serving God. Share your experiences of serving with each other and how God has strengthened you in the process.

Take some time to read through Isaiah 41 and reflect on the themes of God's sovereignty and faithfulness. Thank Him for His promise to strengthen and empower those who serve Him.

DAY 12: STRENGTH FOR SERVANTS - PART 02.

"If they obey and serve him, they shall spend their days in prosperity, and their years in pleasures." - Job 36:11.

Obedience to God and service to Him bring pleasure and joy to our lives. In contrast, disobedience and rebellion bring pain and suffering. Job is an excellent example of this truth. Though he experienced a difficult season of affliction at the hands of Satan, before that time, God referred to him as "My servant Job." As a result, Job was a mighty man on earth and the wealthiest person in the East.

However, Job became sick and weak when Satan afflicted him, feeling broken and sorrowful. Despite this, he held on to God and even prayed for his friends. As a result, God restored his strength, and he lived for another 140 years, even seeing his third generation. It is remarkable how much strength it takes to live up to the age of 90, let alone 200. So, what was Job's secret to living a long and robust life?

He feared God, served Him as a lifestyle, and hated evil. If we want strength and longevity, we must follow in Job's footsteps and make serving God a priority in our lives.

Prayer:
Lord,
I know disobedience and rebellion bring pain, but obedience and service to You bring happiness. Help me to serve You as a lifestyle, and grant me the strength and wisdom to live a long and fulfilling life. May my actions and thoughts be guided by deep fear and respect for You, and may I hate evil in all its forms. Thank You for Your love and grace and the opportunity to serve You.
Amen.

READING: Job 36:1-33.

Reflection:
How has actively serving God brought renewal and strength to your life?

In what ways do you struggle to prioritize serving God and furthering His kingdom?

How can you identify and utilize the specific gifts and talents that God has given you for service?

How does serving God and His kingdom impact your physical, emotional, and spiritual well-being?
How can you prioritize serving God and furthering His kingdom daily?

DAY 13: QUIET TIME TO RECEIVE STRENGTH - PART 01.

"For thus saith the Lord GOD, the Holy One of Israel; in returning and rest shall ye be saved; in quietness and confidence shall be your strength: and ye would not." - Isaiah 30:15

Taking time to be quiet and still our inner selves allows us to focus on God and His Word, which helps to renew and strengthen us. It will enable us to clear our minds and hearts of the distractions and noise of the world and instead fill ourselves with the peace and guidance of God.

When we engage in quiet time with God, we can also use it to pray and communicate with Him. We can bring our needs and concerns to Him and seek His wisdom and direction. As we pour out our hearts to Him, He fills us with His Spirit and strength.

Quiet time with God can take various forms, such as prayer, meditation, reading and studying the Bible, or simply sitting still in His presence. It can be a set time each day, or it can be spontaneous moments throughout the day. It is essential to make it a regular part of our routine and prioritize it above the noise and distractions of the world.

In our busy and often chaotic lives, quiet time with God is essential for maintaining emotional and spiritual strength. It helps us to stay grounded in His love and purpose for our lives and empowers us to face the challenges and struggles that come our way. So make time to be quiet with God, and experience the strength and peace that only He can provide.

Prayer:
Lord,
I know that the world is full of noise and distractions, and
it can be easy to become overwhelmed and exhausted. But
I also know that you offer a way out through Quiet Time,
where I can still the noise of my inner person and hear
your voice. Please give me the discipline and grace to
make Quiet Time a priority in my life so that I may receive
strength from you.
Amen.

READING: Isaiah 30:1-33.

Reflection:
What does "quiet time" with God mean to you?

How do you make time for quiet time in your daily routine?

What benefits have you experienced from spending quiet time with God?

How do you stay focused during your quiet time with God?

In what ways has quiet time with God helped you to face challenges and struggles in your life?

DAY 14: QUIET TIME TO RECEIVE STRENGTH - PART2.

"But they that wait upon the LORD shall renew their strength; they shall mount up with wings as eagles; they shall run, and not be weary, and they shall walk, and not faint." - Isaiah 40:31

Waiting upon the Lord is one crucial aspect of the Christian faith. Waiting on God means being patient while still keeping your expectations alive. It also means taking quiet time away from the world's distractions and noise, focusing on God, and listening for His guidance. It can often involve fasting as a way to seek God with greater intensity and clarity. Yes, even when it feels like God is taking too long to answer your prayers or fulfill His promises.

Many people today are overwhelmed and exhausted from trying to achieve their goals and fulfill their dreams through human strength. But when we wait on God, we receive clarity and direction from Him, and He goes before us to make our path straight and smooth. As we follow His lead, we can experience a level of peace and joy that helps sustain and strengthen us, even in the midst of challenges and difficulties. So if you want to experience lasting strength and fulfillment in your life, prioritize waiting on the Lord. Those who prioritize waiting on God will find that their strength is renewed.

Prayer:
Dear Lord,
I thank you for your abundant grace and love. I confess
that I have not always waited upon you as I should, but I
ask for your help to change my ways. Please grant me the
determination and discipline to take quiet time away from
the distractions and noise of the world, to focus on you and
hear your voice more clearly. When I wait on you, I know
that you go before me to make my path straight and guide
me toward my destiny. Please help me to trust in your
timing and keep my expectations alive, knowing that you
are faithful and good. May I renew my strength as I wait
upon you, Lord.
Amen.

READING: Isaiah 40:1-31.

Reflection:

When you feel overwhelmed and exhausted, how can waiting on the Lord help you find the strength and clarity you need to continue moving forward?

How does quiet time with God help you to stay grounded in His love and purpose for your life?

How can you prioritize waiting on the Lord in your daily routine?

How can fasting be a helpful tool in seeking God with greater intensity and clarity?

How can waiting on the Lord bring peace and joy that can help sustain and strengthen you amid challenges and difficulties?

DAY 15: RIGHTEOUS STRENGTH - PART 1.

"The wicked flee when no man pursueth: but the righteous are bold as a lion." - Proverbs 28:1.

The idea of righteousness can often be misunderstood or overlooked in modern society. Many people may think that being righteous means following rules or behaving in a certain way. Still, true righteousness goes much deeper than that. It involves a deep sense of right and wrong and a desire to do what is right, not just because it is expected or will bring personal gain, but because it is the right thing to do. This type of righteousness is not just a surface-level behavior but a way of life that comes from the heart.

Living a righteous life has many benefits, both physical and emotional. Solomon, a wise king in the Bible, observed that the righteous are strong. Living a virtuous life can give us emotional and physical strength. When we choose to do what is right, even when it is difficult or goes against our desires, we can tap into a sense of inner strength and peace that can carry us through even the toughest of circumstances.

On the other hand, living a life of evil or wrongdoing can be emotionally exhausting. It can weigh heavily on our conscience and leave us feeling drained and empty. But when we live in fear of the Lord, meaning we have a deep reverence and respect for God, we can find strength and stability. We know that God is always on our side and will guide us in the right direction, giving us the strength and courage to face whatever challenges come our way.

So if you want to be emotionally and physically strong, take a lesson from Solomon and make righteousness a part of your lifestyle. Choose to do what is right, not just because it is expected of you, but because it is the right thing to do. When you live in fear of the Lord and strive to live a righteous life, you will find a sense of inner strength and peace that will carry you through even the toughest of times.

Prayer:
"Dear Lord,
I pray that You will fill me with Your Holy Spirit and guide me on the path of righteousness. Help me to fear You and to live a life that is pleasing to You. Please give me the strength and courage to stand firm against evil and resist temptation. May I be a shining example of Your love and grace to those around me. Thank You for Your constant presence and protection in my life.
In Your holy name, I pray,
Amen."

READING: Psalms 119:100-119

Reflection:
How does true righteousness go beyond just following rules or behaving in a certain way?

What are some of the benefits of living a righteous life?

How does living in fear of the Lord give us strength and stability?

How can making righteousness a part of our lifestyle give us inner strength and peace?
Can you think of a time when choosing to do what is right gave you a sense of inner strength or peace? How did this experience impact you?

DAY 16: RIGHTEOUS STRENGTH - PART 2.

"Ye are of God, little children, and have overcome them: because greater is he that is in you than he that is in the world." - 1 John 4:4.

As believers in Jesus Christ, we have the indwelling presence of God within us, which gives us righteousness and allows us to live a life of righteous actions. This indwelling presence is greater than any external force or obstacle, including Satan and his influence in the world.

The Lord, who is strong and mighty, resides within us and empowers us to be strong in every aspect of our lives.

We are not meant to be weak or be overcome by any obstacle; instead, we are meant to thrive and overcome through the strength and power of the Lord within us. This divine strength is evident in the Psalms, where the Lord is described as the King of glory, strong and mighty in battle.

If this same strong and powerful God is within us, we, too, can be strong and victorious in every area of our lives. Therefore, let us embrace the indwelling presence of God and the righteousness it brings, allowing us to live a life of strength and victory. Let us stand firm in the strength of the Lord, knowing that He is greater than any challenge we may face.

Prayer:
Lord,
Let Your Presence in me result in Supernatural Strength that dissolves all weakness in me. I pray that Your strength will flow through me and empower me to overcome any challenges that come my way. I pray that I will be a vessel of Your strength and that Your strength will be perfected in my weakness. I trust in Your power and grace to sustain me and give me the strength I need to fulfill Your purpose for my life.
Amen.

READING: Psalms 24:1-10.

Reflection:
What specific challenges or obstacles are you facing in your life right now? How can you rely on the strength of the Lord to overcome them?

In what ways have you experienced the indwelling presence of God and the strength it brings to your life?

How can you actively cultivate a stronger sense of the Lord's presence and strength within you daily?

Have you ever struggled with feeling weak or overcome by a challenge? How did you find strength and victory in the Lord during that time?

How can you encourage and support others in finding strength and victory through the indwelling presence of God?

DAY 17: SPEAK STRENGTH - PART 1

"Beat your plowshares into swords, and your pruning hooks into spears: let the weak say, I am strong." - Joel 3:10.

To be strong, you must first identify areas where you feel weak or vulnerable. It could be a physical, emotional, or spiritual weakness. Once you have recognized these areas, you must speak words of strength and empowerment over yourself. Declare that you are strong in the Lord and the power of His might. Believe that you can overcome any challenges or obstacles that come your way.

In addition to speaking words of strength, it is also important to take action toward becoming stronger. This action could involve seeking help or support from others, seeking out opportunities for growth and development, and engaging in activities or practices that promote physical, emotional, and spiritual well-being.

Remember, the power of your words can have a significant impact on your life. Choose to speak words of strength and empowerment, and you will begin to see positive changes in yourself and your circumstances. As you do this, trust in the Lord to strengthen you and empower you to live a life of victory and abundance.

Prayer:
Lord,
Empower me with Your wisdom and strength to speak only words of life and strength over my life and circumstances. Help me to align my words with Your will and only to say what is true, pure, and right. May the words of my mouth and the meditations of my heart be pleasing to You.
Amen.
READING: Psalms 81:1-16.

Reflection:
Take a moment to reflect on areas where you feel weak or vulnerable. These could be physical, emotional, or spiritual weaknesses.

Make a list of affirmations or declarations of strength to speak over yourself. Examples might include: "I am strong in the Lord and the power of His might," "I am capable and equipped to overcome any challenge that comes my way," or "I am emotionally and spiritually resilient."

Take action to address your weaknesses and become stronger. This might involve seeking help or support from others, seeking out opportunities for growth and development, or engaging in activities or practices that promote physical, emotional, and spiritual well-being.

Practice speaking your affirmations or declarations of strength daily. Consider writing them down and placing them in a visible location as a reminder to recite them regularly.

Trust in the Lord to strengthen you and empower you to live a life of victory and abundance. Believe that He is working to help you overcome any weaknesses and become the person He has called you to be.

DAY 18: GOD'S HAND OF STRENGTH - PART 1.

"With whom my hand shall be established: mine arm also shall strengthen him." - Ps89:21.

David was a man who enjoyed a divine relationship with God in his life. This relationship is evident from his "hall-of-fame" status and the fact that God made a covenant to retain the throne of Israel in his lineage. Even Jesus, the Son of God, came from David's family line.

One of the keys to David's success and strength was his commitment to do whatever God told him to do. He was a man of prayer and praise, dedicating himself to these practices seven times and three times a day, respectively. In addition to these spiritual disciplines, David was also a warrior who fought battles throughout his life. This combination of spiritual dedication and physical strength contributed to his unusual success.

Those who lay down their lives at the feet of Jesus receive His life into them. As believers in Jesus (or Christians), we have the opportunity to receive His unweary nature and constant strength. If we walk with Him and follow His lead, we can count on the strength and guidance of the unweary Jesus in our lives. This strength is a powerful and transformative experience that can lead us to live lives of unusual exploits and success, just like David.

Prayer:
Lord,
I pray I will have the strength and determination to follow Your will and walk closely with You. I pray that Your presence in my life will give me the strength and courage to face any challenges that come my way. Help me to draw on Your strength and use it to serve You and fulfill Your purpose for my life.
Amen.

READING: Psalms 89:1-52.

Reflection:

How does having a relationship with God contribute to our strength and success in life?

How can you cultivate a stronger relationship with God and draw on His strength in your daily life?

How can we follow David's example and seek spiritual dedication and physical strength in our lives?

How has Jesus's unweary nature and constant strength impacted your life?

How can you apply the principles of prayer, praise, and following Jesus's lead in your own life to experience His strength and guidance?

DAY 19: GOD'S HAND OF STRENGTH - PART 2.

"If I speak of strength, lo, he is strong: and if of judgment, who shall set me a time to plead?" - Job 9:19.

Believers need to understand and internalize the truth that God is present within them. This single truth has the power to transform their lives for the better. When we recognize that God is within us, we are unbeatable, unending in strength, and powerful beyond measure.

The Bible teaches us that God is Omnipotent or all-powerful. Omnipotent means that His strength is incomprehensible to us. It is important to note that everything we desire has already been given to us (2 Peter 1:3). However, these things only manifest through our knowledge of and faith in them.

This verse tells us that God has given us everything we need for a godly life through His divine power. We can all agree that strength is necessary for living. The verse also says that this power only manifests through our knowledge of God and His call to glory and virtue. When we understand that God has deposited strength within us through His presence, we can begin to tap into it and use it to our advantage.

Prayer:
Lord,
I know that inside me, You have deposited Your strength. I connect to it now, and I ask that You help me tap into that strength more and more each day. I pray that as I seek to grow in my knowledge of You, I will also grow in my understanding of the strength available to me through Your presence. Help me rely on You and Your strength in all things, and give me the courage and faith to face every challenge with confidence, knowing that You are with me and that Your strength is made perfect in my weakness. Amen.

READING: Job 9:1-35.

Reflection:
Reflect on a time when you felt weak or vulnerable. How did you overcome this weakness or vulnerability?

Think about an area where you currently feel weak or vulnerable. What steps can you take to speak words of strength and empowerment over yourself in this area?

Consider incorporating spiritual disciplines, such as prayer and praise, into your daily routine. How might these practices help you tap into the strength and power of God in your life?

Think about ways you can take action to become stronger in your physical, emotional, and spiritual well-being. What steps can you take to make progress in these areas? Reflect on the power of your words. How have the words you have spoken over yourself and others impacted your life? How can you be more mindful of the words you speak in the future?

DAY 20: GOD'S HAND OF STRENGTH - PART 3.

"I will seek that which was lost, and bring again that which was driven away, and will bind up that which was broken, and will strengthen that which was sick: but I will destroy the fat and the strong; I will feed them with judgment." - Ezekiel 34:16

God is a God of restoration. He is always ready and willing to restore anything that has been lost, including our strength. Whether physical, emotional, spiritual, intellectual, or financial strength, God can bring restoration and healing. The Bible says that God will bind up the broken and strengthen the sick. This is a promise that we can hold onto and remind God of when we feel weak and need restoration.

God is not afraid to be challenged by His children, as long as it is based on His Word. He is always ready to prove His Word and show us His power. We can stand up and remind God of His promises, knowing He is a God of restoration and healing.

To experience the fullness of God's restoration, we must seek Him and make room for Him to work in our lives. This may mean setting aside time for quiet reflection and prayer or seeking support and guidance from other believers. Regardless of our specific steps, the key is to keep our focus on God and His ability to bring restoration and healing. As we draw near to Him, we can trust that He will bring strength and renewal to every aspect of our lives.

Prayer:
Dear Lord,
I come to you today with a heart full of gratitude and a mind full of faith. I know that you are the God of restoration and that nothing is impossible for you. I stand on your Word and claim your promise of healing and strength for my life. I believe you can bind up that which is broken and strengthen that which is sick. I ask for your divine intervention in my life, and I pray that you restore my health and strength in Jesus' name. I trust in your goodness and unfailing love, and I know you will work everything out for my good. Thank you for your faithfulness and your grace.
Amen.

READING: Ezekiel 34:1-31.

Reflection:
Take some time to reflect on areas where you feel weak or need restoration. Write down any specific areas that come to mind.

Consider reaching out to a trusted Christian friend or mentor to share about these areas and ask for prayer and support.

Spend some time in prayer, asking God to restore and heal the areas of your life that need it. Remind Him of His promise to bind up the broken and strengthen the sick.

Commit to seeking God regularly, setting aside time for quiet reflection and prayer. This may involve finding a quiet place to spend time with God or joining a small group or Bible study.
Consider seeking support and guidance from other believers who can encourage and pray with you. Sharing your struggles with others can be a powerful way to receive strength and support.

Trust in God's ability to restore and heal every aspect of your life. As you draw near to Him, keep your focus on His power and faithfulness, and watch as He brings strength and renewal to every aspect of your life.

DAY 21: GOD'S HAND OF STRENGTH - PART 4.

"Thou, O king, art a king of kings: for the God of heaven hath given thee a kingdom, power, and strength, and glory." - Daniel 2:37.

Daniel 2:37 is a powerful verse highlighting the importance of understanding where true strength comes from. In this passage, Daniel speaks to King Nebuchadnezzar, who was known to be a strong and influential king. However, Daniel makes it clear to the king that all of his strength and power came from God, not from himself.

Nebuchadnezzar would later learn this lesson the hard way after he bragged about the greatness of Babylon, saying, "This great Babylon which my might has built." In response, God removed him from the throne and left him in the wilderness, eating grass like an animal for seven years. This lesson serves as a reminder that God does not need us; instead, we need Him and His strength.
It's important to recognize that everyone in the Old Testament, including King Nebuchadnezzar, was considered less than John the Baptist. However, as believers in Jesus Christ, we are told that we are even greater than John the Baptist. We are also called kings and priests, which means that we will also need the strength of God to fulfill our roles and His purposes for our lives. True strength does not come from our power or might but from the spirit of God. It does not come from eating healthy foods or working out but from seeking and relying on the strength of God.

Prayer:
Lord,
I thank You for Your strength that is available to me. I
know I am not strong in and of myself, but I can do all
things through Christ, who gives me strength. Help me to
remember that my strength comes from You and to rely on
You in all things. Give me the courage and determination
to face whatever challenges may come my way, knowing
that Your strength is made perfect in my weakness. Thank
You for Your presence and power in my life.
In Jesus' Name,
Amen.

READING: Daniel 2:1-49.

Reflection:
Reflect on when you relied on your strength to accomplish something but ultimately realized that you needed God's strength to succeed. How did this experience change your perspective on where true strength comes from?

Think about a current challenge or obstacle in your life. How can you rely on God's strength to overcome it?

Consider the role of a king or priest. How can you rely on God's strength as you fulfill your responsibilities and serve others daily?

Make a list of ways to actively seek and rely on God's strength in your daily life. This could include prayer, reading the Bible, worshipping, or participating in a small group.

DAY 22: GOD'S HAND OF STRENGTH - PART 5.

"Then there came again and touched me one like the appearance of a man, and he strengthened me, And said, O man greatly beloved, fear not: peace be unto thee, be strong, yea, be strong. And when he had spoken unto me, I was strengthened, and said, Let my Lord speak; for thou hast strengthened me." - Daniel 10:18-19.

Daniel's encounter with the angel is a powerful reminder of the transformative power of God's presence. We are changed when we encounter God through prayer, fasting, or other spiritual practices. We are given strength, courage, and wisdom that we could not have found on our own. But it is important to note that these encounters are not just for the benefit of the individual. They also have a broader impact on the world around us. As Daniel's encounter showed, God can use his strength and power to bring about change and liberation for others. When God's presence strengthens us, we are better equipped to be a force for good in the world, working to bring justice, healing, and restoration to those around us.

So if you want to be strengthened by God, it's important to seek out opportunities for encounters. Spend time in prayer and meditation, seeking the face of God. Engage in spiritual practices that allow you to connect with the Divine. And be open to the ways that God might reveal Himself to you, whether through the natural world, the words of others, or the inner promptings of the Holy Spirit. As you do, you will find yourself strengthened and empowered to make a difference in the world.

Prayer:
Lord,
I pray that You will empower me to live in fear of You. I pray that I may be more attuned to Your Spirit and ready to receive the strength and revelation that come through a divine encounter with You. Help me be more spiritual and less carnal so that I may be worthy of experiencing Your touch and presence in a powerful way.
I ask for Your grace and guidance in this, Lord.
Amen.

READING: Daniel 10:1-21.

Reflection:
Reflect on a time when you had a powerful encounter with God. What did you experience, and how did it strengthen you?

Think about a current challenge or struggle in your life. How might seeking out an encounter with God help you find strength and guidance in this situation?

Consider how you can create space in your life for encounters with God. This might include setting aside time for prayer and meditation, participating in spiritual practices such as fasting or service, or being open to unexpected moments of encounter.

Take some time to pray and ask God to reveal Himself to you in a powerful way. Ask for His strength and guidance as you navigate the challenges and opportunities in your life.

DAY 23: GOD'S HAND OF STRENGTH - PART 6

"And the hand of the LORD was on Elijah, and he girded up his loins and ran before Ahab to the entrance of Jezreel." - 1 Kings 18:46.

God's strength and power are truly awe-inspiring. There are many examples throughout the Bible of individuals who could tap into this strength and do extraordinary things. One such example is the story of Elijah, a prophet who experienced a time of great famine in Israel. Despite his challenges, including the fact that he had not been eating well and was busy working, Elijah still demonstrated incredible physical strength. When he saw a sign of rain coming, the hand of God came upon him, and he outran a horse.

This display of divine strength is a powerful reminder that our physical strength is limited and often insufficient. While we may try to improve our physical strength through exercise and proper nutrition, God is ultimately the source of true strength. This strength is highlighted in the verse, "Not by might, not by power, but by my Spirit sayeth the Lord of Hosts." Through the power of the Holy Spirit, we can tap into the strength that God has made available to us.

In addition to God's spiritual strength, it is important to remember that He can also restore physical strength. God can restore and renew our physical strength through miraculous healing or simply providing the sustenance and nourishment that our bodies need.

God's strength is truly unparalleled. We can rely on Him to provide us with the strength and power we need to overcome any obstacle or challenge that we may face. Whether spiritual or physical strength, God is always ready and willing to provide it to those who turn to Him in faith.

Prayer:

Lord God,

I pray you would give me the same divine strength and speed you gave Elijah. I know that in my strength, I am limited and weak. But with your power working within me, I can do all things. Help me trust in your strength and not rely on my abilities. Give me the courage and determination to run my race with endurance, knowing that you are with me every step of the way. I pray that I experience your hand upon me, empowering me to do what needs to be done. Thank you for your faithfulness and ability to work miracles in my life.

In Jesus' name,

Amen.

READING: 1 Kings 18:1-46.

Reflection:
Reflect on a time when you experienced God's strength in your life. How did this experience strengthen your faith and trust in Him?

Think about a current challenge or obstacle in your life. How can you rely on God's strength to overcome it?

Consider how God has provided for your physical and spiritual needs. Take some time to thank Him for His faithfulness and provision.
Make a list of ways that you can tap into the strength and power of the Holy Spirit in your daily life. This might include reading the Bible, praying, worshiping, or serving others.

DAY 24: STRENGTH BY KNOWING HE IS THERE.

"Be strong and of a good courage, fear not, nor be afraid of them: for the LORD thy God, He it is that doth go with thee; He will not fail thee, nor forsake thee." - Deuteronomy 31:6.

Fear can be a debilitating emotion, causing us to feel weak and powerless. However, as believers in Jesus, we have the opportunity to tap into a source of strength that goes beyond our own physical and emotional capabilities. This strength comes from the presence of God in our lives, as He is omnipotent and able to do all things. When we have faith in His power and presence, we can find hope and strength in any situation, no matter how intimidating it may seem.

Believers need to remember that God is always with us, even in times of fear and uncertainty, as the verse in Deuteronomy 31:6 reminds us. This means that we can have confidence in His protection and provision, knowing He will never leave us to face challenges on our own.
To tap into this source of strength, we must seek a deeper understanding and knowledge of God's presence in our lives. This understanding and knowledge can be achieved through prayer, reading the Bible, and worship and fellowship with other believers. As we draw closer to God and His Word, we will find that our fear is replaced with faith and strength, enabling us to face any challenge with courage and determination.

Prayer:
Lord,
I ask that You give me the strength to overcome fear and replace it with faith. Give me the knowledge of Your Word and the revelation of Your presence that will fill me with confidence and hope to stand strong in the face of any challenge or threat. Help me to remember that I am always in Your presence and that You are Omnipotent and able to protect and defend me.
In Jesus' Name,
Amen.

READING: Deuteronomy 31:1-30.

Reflection:
Reflect on a time when you felt overwhelmed by fear.
How did you find strength and overcome it?

Think about a current fear or worry that you are facing.
How can trust in the presence of God give you hope and
strength to overcome it?

Consider how you can draw closer to God and His Word to
deepen your understanding and knowledge of His presence
in your life. This might include prayer, reading the Bible,
worshiping, or being part of a small group or community
of believers.

Take some time to pray and ask God to reveal Himself to
you in a deeper way. Ask for His strength and protection as
you face any challenges or fears in your life.

DAY 25: STRONG BY REDEMPTION - PART 1.

"Saying with a loud voice, worthy is the Lamb that was slain to receive power, and riches, and wisdom, and strength, and honor, and glory, and blessing." - Revelation 5:12

Revelation 5:12 speaks to the fact that Jesus died for us to obtain certain things for us, including strength. Many people believe that redemption is only related to spiritual matters or that it is something that we will only receive in heaven. However, this verse suggests that Christ obtained strength for us and that it is something that we can claim and use here on earth.

To claim this strength, we must first believe that it is our birthright as children of God. We must confess our right to it and then begin to do things that we may have previously been unable to do due to a lack of strength. It is important to remember that this strength is not something we can gain on our own, but rather it is given to us through Christ and his redemptive work.

Believers must understand the full extent of what Jesus has obtained for us through his death and resurrection. In doing so, we can more fully tap into the strength available to us and live the abundant life God has called us to. So, let us confidently claim the strength that is rightfully ours through Christ and live in the power of his redemption.

Prayer:
Lord, I believe that I am entitled to the strength that Jesus obtained for me through his death. I confess that strength is my portion as a child of God. Help me to begin to do things that I was previously unable to do, and let me experience the fullness of your strength in my life. Amen.

READING: Revelation 5:1-14.

Reflection:
Reflect on the concept of redemption and how it relates to the strength that Jesus obtained for us. How has this understanding impacted your faith and ability to claim and use the strength available to you through Christ?

Think about a specific area of your life where you feel weak or lacking in strength. How can believing in the power of Christ's redemption help you overcome this weakness?

Consider how you can actively claim and utilize the strength available to you through Christ's redemptive work. This might include prayer, Bible reading, worshiping, or serving others.

Take some time to pray and ask God to reveal the full extent of what He has obtained for you through Christ's death and resurrection. Ask for His strength and power to be made manifest in your life.

DAY 26: STRENGTH IN TRIALS - PART 1

"God is our refuge and strength, an ever-present help in trouble." - Psalm 46:1

It cannot be easy to find strength when we are facing trials and challenges in life. It's natural to feel overwhelmed, discouraged, and even hopeless. But the good news is that we have a God who is bigger than any problem we may face, and he can give us the strength we need to get through even the most difficult circumstances.

One of the key ways we can find strength in trials is by turning to God's Word and seeking guidance and encouragement. The Bible contains passages that offer hope, comfort, and strength to those facing difficult situations. The verse for today reminds us that God is always with us, providing us with the strength and protection we need to endure whatever challenges come our way.

Another way to find strength in trials is by seeking support from others. Whether through prayer, fellowship with other believers, or having someone to talk to. A supportive network of people around us can make a big difference in how we cope with difficult circumstances.

Finally, it's important to remember that trials can ultimately serve as a source of growth and strength. We become stronger and more resilient when we face challenges and overcome them. So even though trials may be difficult and painful in the moment, they can ultimately help us grow and become the person God has created us to be.

In conclusion, finding strength in trials is possible with the help of God and supportive relationships. By turning to God's Word and seeking support from others, we can find the strength we need to endure and overcome even the most difficult circumstances.

Prayer:
Dear God, I am facing a difficult trial and need your strength to get through it. I know you are bigger than any problem I may face, and I trust your goodness and love. Please give me the courage and determination to endure this trial and to find hope and purpose in it. Please help me to turn to your Word for guidance and to seek support from others as I navigate this challenge. Above all, help me remember that you are with me and working everything for my good.
Thank you for your faithfulness and your never-ending love.
Amen.

Reading: Psalm 27:1

Reflection:
Reflect on a time when you faced a difficult trial and found the strength to get through it. What helped you find strength in that situation?

Think about a current trial or challenge you are facing. How can turning to God's Word and seeking support from others help you find the strength you need to endure and overcome it?

Consider how trials can ultimately serve as a source of growth and strength. How can you view your current trial as an opportunity for growth and resilience?

Ask God to give you the strength and guidance you need to face your current trial.

DAY 27: STRENGTH IN TRIALS - PART 2.

"Do not be anxious about anything, but in every situation, by prayer and petition, with thanksgiving, present your requests to God. And the peace of God, which transcends all understanding, will guard your hearts and your minds in Christ Jesus." - Philippians 4:6-7

One way to find strength in trials is by focusing on what you can control. It can be easy to become overwhelmed by a difficult situation, especially if it feels like everything is out of your control. But you can gain a sense of empowerment and agency by focusing on the things you can control, such as your thoughts, actions, and attitude. This can help you feel more in control of the situation and better equipped to handle it.

Another way to find strength in trials is by practicing gratitude. When going through tough times, it can be easy to focus on all the negative aspects of the situation and lose sight of the good things in our lives. Practicing gratitude can help us reframe our perspective and focus on the blessings and positives, even amid difficulty. This can help us find hope and strength to persevere.

Prayer:
Dear Lord, I am facing a difficult trial and struggling to find the strength I need to get through it. I know many things are beyond my control, and I feel overwhelmed and helpless. Please give me the wisdom and strength to focus on the things I can control and let go of the things that are outside of my control. Please help me to trust in your plan. Please help me to remember that you are with me every step of the way. Give me the courage and determination to persevere through this challenge and find hope and purpose.
Thank you for your never-ending love and grace.
Amen.

Reading: Psalm 118:5:

Reflection:
Reflect on a time when focusing on what you could control helped you find strength in a difficult trial. How did this approach empower you and help you cope with the situation?

Think about a current trial or challenge you are facing. How can focusing on what you can control help you find strength and resilience in this situation?

Consider how practicing gratitude can help you find strength and hope in difficult times. How can you actively cultivate gratitude, even amid trial and hardship?

Pray and ask God for the wisdom and strength to focus on what you can control and to practice gratitude in the face of your current trial.

DAY 28: GOD'S STRENGTH IN WEAKNESS.

"But he said to me, 'My grace is sufficient for you, for my power is made perfect in weakness.' Therefore I will boast all the more gladly about my weaknesses, so that Christ's power may rest on me." - 2 Corinthians 12:9

One of the great mysteries of the Christian faith is the idea that God's strength is made perfect in weakness. This concept is exemplified in the story of Paul, who wrote about his own struggles with weakness in the verse reading for today. Paul says the grace of God is sufficient enough.

What does it mean that God's strength is made perfect in weakness? It means that when we are weakest and most vulnerable, God can work most powerfully in and through us. It's not that God needs us to be weak in order to be strong, but rather that when we are weak, we are more reliant on God and more open to his power working in our lives.

This doesn't mean that we should seek out weakness or try to make ourselves weaker. Instead, it means that when we are faced with physical, emotional, or spiritual weakness, we can turn to God and trust in his strength to sustain us. In doing so, we can experience the fullness of his grace and power in our lives.

So if you are feeling weak or vulnerable today, know that this is an opportunity for God to work in a powerful way in your life. Don't be afraid to admit your weakness and ask for God's help. Trust in his strength to sustain you and see what he can do through your weakness.

Prayer:
Dear God, I feel weak and vulnerable right now, and I need your strength to sustain me. I know that your strength is made perfect in weakness, and I trust in your ability to work powerfully in my life, even in my darkest moments. Please give me the courage to admit my weakness and to turn to you for help. Please help me to rely on your strength and to experience the fullness of your grace and power in my life. Thank you for loving me and for being my constant source of strength and encouragement. Amen.

Reading: Psalm 73:26

Reflection:

Reflect on a time when you felt weak or vulnerable. How did you turn to God for strength in that situation? What could you have done differently to rely on God's strength if you didn't?

Write down a list of areas where you feel weak or vulnerable. Take each one to God in prayer, asking for his strength and grace to sustain you.

Spend some time meditating on 2 Corinthians 12:9. How does this verse speak to you in your current situation? What does it mean that God's strength is made perfect in weakness?

Consider creating a personal prayer journal to record your prayers and reflections on God's strength in weakness. Use this resource to reflect on and see how God has sustained you in difficult times.

DAY 29: TRUSTING IN GOD'S STRENGTH.

"And we know that in all things God works for the good of those who love him, who have been called according to his purpose." - Romans 8:28

One of the key ways we can find strength in times of trial is by trusting in God and relying on his power to sustain us. This can be a difficult thing to do, especially when we are feeling weak and vulnerable. But the good news is that God is faithful and always ready to provide us with the help we need.

So how can we trust in God's strength and find the courage to rely on him in times of trial? Here are a few things to consider:

Remember that God is bigger than any problem you may be facing. No matter how difficult the situation may seem, God is able to work things out for your good.
Turn to God's Word for guidance and encouragement. The Bible is full of verses that offer hope and strength in times of difficulty.

Seek support from others. Whether through prayer, fellowship with other believers, or simply having someone to talk to, having a supportive network of people around us can make a big difference in how we cope with difficult circumstances.

Trust in God's faithfulness. God is always with you and is never going to abandon you. Lean on his promises and trust that he will see you through the trial.

Trusting in God's strength can be difficult, but it is essential for finding the courage and resilience we need to get through tough times. Remember that God is with you every step of the way and is ready to provide you with the strength you need to persevere.

Prayer:
Dear God, I am struggling to trust in your strength and rely on you during this trial. I feel weak and uncertain and don't know how to find the courage and resilience I need to get through this. Please help me to turn to you and to trust in your faithfulness and love. Please give me the strength to turn to your Word for guidance and to seek support from others as I navigate this challenge. Above all, help me remember that you are with me every step of the way and that you are working everything for my good.
Thank you for your never-ending love and grace.
Amen.

Reading: Proverbs 3:5-6

Reflection:

Reflect on when you faced a trial or challenge and had to trust God's strength to get through it. Write about the experience and how you found the courage and resilience to persevere.

Make a list of your favorite verses in the Bible that offer hope and strength in times of difficulty. Choose one verse from the list and meditate on it, asking God to give you the strength and courage you need to face your current trial.

Practice gratitude by writing down three things you are grateful for each day, even amid a trial. This can help you refocus on the blessings in your life and find hope and strength to persevere.

Spend time in prayer, asking God to give you the strength and courage you need to trust in him and rely on his power. Thank him for his faithfulness and his never-ending love and grace.

DAY 30: WHY STRENGTH?

"And they went forth and preached everywhere, the Lord working with them, and confirming the word with signs following. Amen." -
Mark 16:20.

The concept of strength is important in the Bible and has been a topic of discussion throughout this month. We have been seeking guidance from God's Word on strengthening ourselves and others who may be struggling spiritually, physically, or emotionally. But what is the significance of all this? Why is strength such a big deal?

To understand the importance of strength, consider the Kingdom of God, which encompasses both the spiritual and physical aspects of our lives. There are numerous examples of people, both in the Bible and in real life, who demonstrated great physical and spiritual strength. One such person was a man named Jack Coe, who was known for his incredible faith and ability to perform miracles, including removing cancer from people's bodies. Despite his powerful faith and miraculous abilities, Coe's life ended suddenly at age 38. He famously said, "God gave me a Message and a horse to carry the Message. I still have the Message, but the horse is tired." This statement speaks to the fact that Coe was physically exhausted and unable to continue carrying out his mission.

The story of Jack Coe serves as a reminder that strength is necessary to fulfill our purpose on earth. The disciples of Jesus, for example, were called to take the Gospel from place to place, which required a great deal of physical and spiritual strength. Similarly, those who are called to be athletes must also possess the physical strength to excel in their sport. Ultimately, strength is a vital component of our destiny and plays a crucial role in enabling us to achieve our goals and fulfill our potential.

Prayer:
Dear Lord, I come before you today asking for your strength to guide me on my path and help me fulfill my destiny. I know that I am not alone and that with your help, I can overcome any obstacle and achieve all that you have planned for me. Please give me the courage and determination to stay focused on my goals and persevere through the challenges that may come my way. Help me trust in your plan for my life and rely on your strength when I feel weak or uncertain.

Thank you for the gift of your love and guidance.

Amen.

READING: Mark 16:1-20.

Reflection:
Reflect on your life and consider what goals or missions you feel called to fulfill. How does strength play a role in achieving these goals?

Consider reaching out to a friend or family member who may be going through a difficult time and offer them encouragement and support. How can you be a source of strength for them?

Take some time to pray and ask God to give you the strength you need to fulfill your purpose and achieve your goals.

Consider incorporating activities or practices into your routine to help you build physical or spiritual strength, such as exercise or daily Bible study.

CONCLUSION

We hope this 30-day devotional on *"Finding strength in God's Word"* has been a blessing and encouragement to you. As you have explored various aspects of strength and how they relate to your faith and walk with God, we pray that you have been strengthened and empowered to face life's challenges with courage and resilience. Remember that God is always with you, ready to provide you with the strength and guidance you need to get through any trial. Trust in his faithfulness and love, and seek out his Word and fellowship with others for support and encouragement. And never forget that God's strength is made perfect in weakness. When you feel weak and vulnerable, turn to God and rely on his strength to sustain you. He will give you the courage and resilience to persevere and find hope and purpose in even the most difficult circumstances. We pray that you will continue to grow in your faith and reliance on God and experience his love, grace, and power more deeply as you trust in him for strength. May God bless you and keep you always.
Amen.

Here are a few more verses from the Bible that you continue to read on finding strength in God's word:

- *Philippians 4:13: "I can do all things through Christ who gives me strength."*

- *Psalm 27:14: "Wait for the Lord; be strong and take heart and wait for the Lord."*

- *Isaiah 40:31: "But those who hope in the Lord will renew their strength. They will soar on wings like eagles; they will run and not grow weary, they will walk and not be faint."*

- *Ephesians 6:10: "Finally, be strong in the Lord and in his mighty power."*

- *1 Peter 5:7: "Cast all your anxiety on him because he cares for you."*

We hope these verses continue to encourage and strengthen you as you rely on God for guidance and strength.

THANK YOU

Thank you for completing this 30-day devotional on ***"Finding Strength In God's Word"***. We hope this devotional has been a blessing and encouragement to you as you have sought to grow in your faith and reliance on God.

If you're looking for more resources to help you grow your faith and deepen your relationship with God, we invite you to check out some of our other devotionals. Here are a few that we recommend:

30 Day Devotional On "The Word For Expectant Mothers"

30 Day Devotional For Strength in difficult times

30 Day Devotional For Dealing With Loss

The Christian's Guide to Dealing With Addiction

Dealing With Anxiety, Doubt and Worry

Quiet Time With God Each Night (Before Going off to Sleep)

Quiet time with God Each Morning (Before Starting Your Day)

Finding Our Way Back to God

Christian's Guide to Seeking the Fruit of the Womb

ABOUT THE AUTHOR

Maddie T. Kabba is a Christian author, teacher, and founder of Christian Devotionals & Guidebooks LLC. She was born in Cameroon and has lived in various countries throughout her life, including the United States where she currently resides with her family.

Maddie has a Bachelor in Education and is dedicated to sharing the message of the Christian faith with others. She is the founder of a company that produces high-quality devotion materials and guidebooks to help people grow in their faith and deepen their relationship with God.

Maddie is a driven and motivated individual who is committed to making a positive impact in the world and helping others grow in their faith. In her spare time, she enjoys reading, traveling, and spending time with her family.

You can reach Maddie at *kabba.t.maddie@christdevotionals.com*

Made in the USA
Las Vegas, NV
07 December 2024

13534705R00059